What Happens When Wind Blows?

What Happens When
Wind
Blows?

Daphne Butler

RSVP

RAINTREE
STECK-VAUGHN
PUBLISHERS
The Steck-Vaughn Company

Austin, Texas

Published by Raintree Steck-Vaughn Publishers, an imprint of Steck-Vaughn Company

Library of Congress Cataloging-in-Publication Data

Butler, Daphne, 1945–
    What happens when wind blows? / Daphne Butler.
        p.   cm. — (What happens when—?)
    Includes index.
    ISBN 0-8172-4153-1
    1. Winds—Juvenile literature. 2. Weather—Juvenile literature.
[1. Winds. 2. Weather.] I. Title. II. Series: Butler, Daphne,
1945– What happens when—?
QC931.4.B87   1996
551.5'18—dc20   95-13660
                                            CIP
                                          AC

Printed and bound in Singapore
1 2 3 4 5 6 7 8 9 0 99 98 97 96 95

Contents

Wind and Weather

Wind is always changing. It brings rain, dries the wash, and makes your ears cold in the winter. Sometimes there is no wind at all. Other times it's tugging at your clothes and messing up your hair.

Yet it can blow steadily from one
direction for weeks and weeks.

No Wind at All

When no wind blows, the air is very
still. Smoke, balloons, and bubbles
drift slowly upward.

Not a leaf stirs.

Wind Clouds

High above, thin **wisps** of clouds show that the weather is changing.

Soon a wind will blow. Tomorrow, the sky may be cloudy. Perhaps it will rain.

A Fresh Breeze

As the wind gets stronger, leaves rustle, and flags wave.

Smoke from chimneys is swept away by the **breeze**, and kites soar in the wind. Sailboats begin to glide through the water.